MACDONALD STARTERS

Snakes

Macdonald/London

About Macdonald Starters

Macdonald Starters are vocabulary controlled information books for young children. More than ninety per cent of the words in the text will be in the reading vocabulary of the vast majority of young readers. Word and sentence length have also been carefully controlled.

Key new words associated with the topic of each book are repeated with picture explanations in the Starters dictionary at the end. The dictionary can also be used as an index for teaching children to look things up.

Teachers and experts have been consulted on the content and accuracy of the books.

Illustrated by: Lorna Paull

Editors: Peter Usborne, Su Swallow, Jennifer Vaughan

Reading consultant: Donald Moyle, author of *The Teaching of Reading* and senior lecturer in education at Edge Hill College of Education

Chairman, teacher advisory panel: F. F. Blackwell, general inspector for schools, London Borough of Croydon, with responsibility for primary education

Teacher panel: Elizabeth Wray, Loveday Harmer, Lynda Snowdon, Joy West

© Macdonald and Company (Publishers) Limited 1971

Made and printed in Great Britain by Purnell & Sons Limited Paulton, nr Bristol

First published 1971 by Macdonald and Company (Publishers) Limited St Giles House 49-50 Poland Street London W1

The snake lies in the sun.
The sun keeps the snake warm.

Now the snake wriggles along.
It feels the ground
with its tongue.
2

This is the snake's head.
It has no eyelids.
It has two big teeth in front.
It can fold the teeth back.

The snake finds a mouse.
It bites the mouse.
Poison from the big teeth
kills the mouse quickly.

4

The snake swallows the mouse.

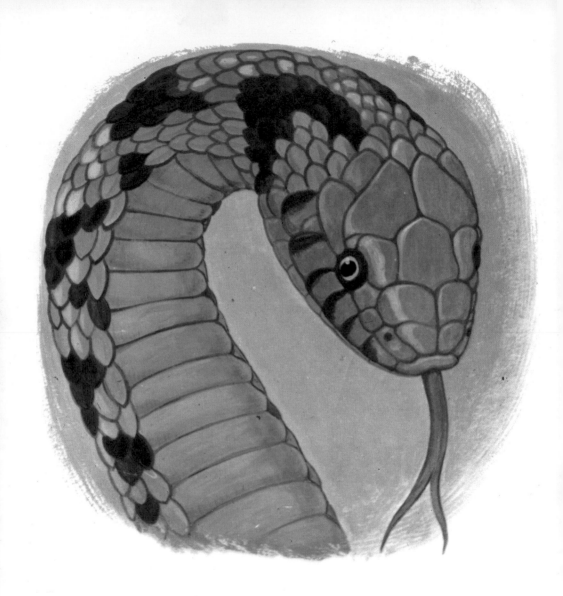

The snake has a scaly skin.
The scales on its back are small.
The scales are bigger underneath.

6

Snakes often grow a new skin.
Then the old skin comes off.

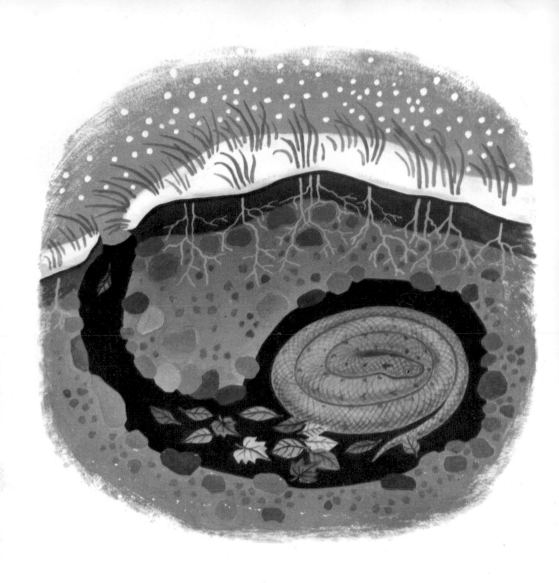

In winter snakes find a hiding place.
They stay asleep.

Many snakes lay eggs.
Baby snakes soon come out.

This is a rattlesnake.
It lives in America.
It rattles when it is afraid.

This rattlesnake lives in a desert.
It wriggles sideways very quickly.

11

This is a python.
It lives in India.
It is very long.
It waits in a tree.

The python catches a goat.
It winds round the goat.
The goat cannot breathe.

13

This is a sea snake.
Sea snakes have flat tails.
Their tails help them swim.
They often eat fish.

This snake lives in trees.
It can glide to another tree.
It makes its body flat.
It is called a flying snake.

This snake eats eggs.
It swallows the inside of the egg.
It spits out the shell.

16

This snake is a cobra.
It lives in India.
It can make its neck very big.
It sometimes bites men.

17

This is a spitting cobra.
It can spit poison.

This man is a snake charmer.
He keeps his cobra in a basket.

Some people love snakes.
This man kept pet snakes.
They did not bite him.
20

Some animals hunt snakes.
The mongoose hunts snakes.
Some birds eat snakes.

See for yourself
Go to the zoo.
How many snakes from this book
can you find?

22

Starter's **Snakes** words

tongue
(page 2)

skin
(page 7)

teeth
(page 3)

egg
(page 9)

swallow
(page 5)

rattlesnake
(page 10)

scales
(page 6)

America
(page 10)

23

desert
(page 11)

goat
(page 13)

python
(page 12)

sea snake
(page 14)

India
(page 12)

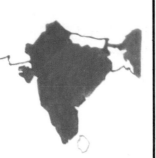

tail
(page 14)

tree
(page 12)

flying snake
(page 15)

glide
(page 15)

bite
(page 17)

shell
(page 16)

snake charmer
(page 19)

cobra
(page 17)

basket
(page 19)

neck
(page 17)

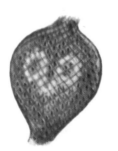

mongoose
(page 21)